Ten

Sentience changed *everything*...

We just weren't paying attention

Whickwithy

Ten

Published by Whickwithy

whickwithy@gmail.com

ISBN: 978-1-7348221-7-5

Ten by Whickwithy

First published Spring 2023
Latest edition Summer 2023

Previous efforts:
Sentience
A Sentient Perspective
Beauty & Fiction
MillenniumBook 6
The Sentient Struggle For Transformation
This And That
The Bane of Mankind

An animal's life is what it was given. Human life is what we make of it. Prehuman life is all that we have attained, so far.

"Education of the mind without education of the heart is no education at all" (it is *prehuman*)
   -Aristotle

"When will our consciences grow so tender that we will act to prevent human misery rather than avenge it?"
   - Eleanor Roosevelt

Answer: when we become human.

I like very much that this, my last book, is about the same length as *Howl*.

"The smell of a world that is burned"
  - Jimi Hendrix

"Power at its most vicious is a riposte to powerlessness."
  - Simone de Beauvoir

"Great minds discuss ideas; average minds discuss events; small minds discuss people."
  - Eleanor Roosevelt

"Sure he (Fred Astaire) was great, but don't forget that Ginger Rogers did everything he did, ...backwards and in high heels."
  - Bob Thaves, "Frank and Ernest" comic strip

"Darkness cannot drive out darkness; only light can do that. Hate cannot drive out hate; only love can do that."
  - Martin Luther King, Jr.

"And nothing natural is evil"
  -Marcus Aurelius

"The unexamined life is not worth living"
"Let he that would move the world first move himself"
"From the deepest desires often come the deadliest hate"
  - Socrates
  (These seem to be my call signs. Incredible.)

"History is a pack of lies about events that never happened told by people who weren't there."
  - George Santayana

"The reason why the world lacks unity, and lies broken and in heaps, is, because man is disunited with himself."
  -Ralph Waldo Emerson

"What lies behind you and what lies in front of you, pales in comparison to what lies inside of you."
  -Ralph Waldo Emerson

"And that's the thing
Do you recognize the bell of truth
When you hear it ring"
  -Leon Russell

"For truth is always strange; stranger than fiction."
  -Lord Byron

"I've got some words to say about the way we live today.
Why can't we learn to love each other. *It's time to learn a new face for the whole world wide human race*."
  -Leon Russell

"We are what we repeatedly do. Therefore, excellence is not an act, but a habit."
  -Aristotle
  (Boy, does that apply)

**"A little learning is a dangerous thing
Drink deep, or taste not the Pierian Spring"**
  -Alexander Pope

"There are only two ways to live your life. One is as though nothing is a miracle. The other is as though everything is a miracle."
— Albert Einstein

"It is never too late to be what you might have been."
— George Eliot

"We accept the love we think we deserve."
— Stephen Chbosky

"I saw ten thousand talkers whose tongues were all broken"
  -Bob Dylan

"Once, while Thales was gazing upwards while doing astronomy, he fell into a well. A Thracian serving-girl made fun of him, since he was eager to know the things in the heavens but failed to notice that which was right in front of him."
- Plato
~Thales is often noted as the originator of philosophy

"One who asks a question feels like a fool for a moment. One who refuses to ask a question feels a fool for a lifetime." Or, a sentient race remains a fool for millennia.
-Japanese proverb

Humanity remains a dilettante at sentience, a poser. We're on the threshold of something more, something human.

It is very much like waking from a nightmare to find a dream.

I'd much rather be writing poetry.

It's been a very long, painful road. I am glad it is nearly done.

Past & future

Our self-respect, as a sentient race, is missing in action.

I'm not here to excoriate our past. I've done enough of that. I spent nine books raging at the delusions, confusion, and apathy that humanity developed over the last few millennia.

That was after wondering for forty years what was wrong with humanity and finally figuring it out. I was so wound up by the realization that it took me another eight years to process the outrage and direct the fury into an explanation.

Let me just say this about our past. The phrase, "we are only human" says it all. We will remain an animal in human form until we can say, "Omigoddess! We are human!" with confidence.

There is active resistance to becoming human because of a misunderstanding that goes back at least three millennia, maybe even further. Every human alive is convinced we cannot be more than the mess we currently are.

Why should we expect it to change? We've always been that way.

It is a long convoluted story of blindness.

Who would believe it? Who would think that it is possible that we could rid ourselves completely of the foolishness, brutishness, and insanity that we have always endured and accepted as the best we can do?

"Don't worry. Just a few more millennia and we will grow out of it," the mantra pounds into us. Or, the worse delusion, "Don't worry. Everything will be fine after you are dead." Right.

We will not grow out of it. It is not a training exercise. We are not Pavlov's Dog. Humanity is born to love and convinced over a lifetime that it is not possible to do so. We believe we are too incompetent to become emotionally stable, rational, loving creatures. We are so wrong.

There is active resistance to humanity fulfilling its *natural* compassionate, self-respecting, honorable, dignified state of <u>sentient</u> integrity. The resistance is not due to some mysterious conspiracy but the awful inertia of our animal past. Misperceptions regarding our animal heritage confound us.

And, of course, who would believe it all comes down to a single misconception that we adopted when we first attained sentient thought? It was as inevitable as the tide.

What makes it all so very ridiculous is that it has been right there in front of us all along! It's not that we couldn't see.

We are all aware of it and don blinders. The quandary remains lurking in our subconscious, where we have forced it to remain. Our forced blindness has disabled our sentient consciousness.

We are an animal acting out the part of a human. Our honour, integrity, dignity, compassion, and self-respect need to be unleashed, not regrown. Once we can maintain our self-respect, the rest follow. We can become human, not just act out the part.

We have tolerated, justified, excused, or jollied the prehuman state along all the while. That will not do.

Excuse me. I have to take a deep breath. This is usually where I became derailed in all of the previous books. My fury would take hold. It is truly difficult to articulate something completely new that has never been contemplated before. It is easier to just rage and rant.

In other words, it has been difficult to peer through the blinds.

Worse yet, I would convince myself that we put up with this nonsense for more than three millennia *for no good reason.*

I finally had to admit there *were* good reasons. Those reasons no longer remain.

The obstructions we put in the way of our sentient awareness, the reason for the fear of confronting a sentient reality, are truly momentous and a bit mind-boggling.

We have been a sentient creature attempting to confront its heightened awareness while submitting to its animal circumstances.

There is a good reason it took us so long to realize we can be human right now, not in some far distant, fairy tale future.

The problem was double-edged.

We have had to grow into our sentient awareness a great deal so that we could simultaneously face an issue *and* resolve it. Nothing less is acceptable for a self-respecting sentient race. The issue at hand is also, in itself, double edged.

The inertia caused by the perceptions of the animals that preceded us and a particular confounding situation that is so very difficult to confront has put pause on attaining our sentient state.

It has taken us three millennia to realize that we can overcome the animal's instincts that have defeated us. Keep that phrase is mind. Animal instincts is not a casual phrase. It is a causal phrase.

Because it was beyond our ancient ancestors knowledge and insights to grasp the issue, it has remained buried very deeply. It might as well be in the Marianna Trench.

We have been caught between our sentient awareness and our animal instincts. It has always been a matter of indulging the desire to deflect. We have relied on the subconscious. That was far easier than bringing the issue into the light without resolution.

An animal shunts all confounding situations into its subconscious because it has no choice. An animal can't adapt. When we do the same, we are acting like an animal.

Our sentience faces the consequences, whether we like it or not. Shunting it into the subconscious does not work for a sentient being.

This is exactly where I got stuck in all of my previous books. It is exactly where prehumanity has been stuck for millennia. There is an issue we don't want to face and, yet is is critical.

After about the third book, my rage got the better of me. Why couldn't anyone understand what I was explaining? The fear is rooted so deeply we turn away.

We have made such a mess of it all that it has taken me fifty years to get through it all and perceive our sentience.

This critical issue makes it difficult to inspect our current condition closely. Translating my insights into articulate words just about did me in. Just rant and rave. It's so easy! This time, I will keep my head or I won't right the book.

I could see the insane split personality of humanity. I guess my question is why no one else seems to be able to see it. Even so, it took me a long while to peer through the fog and see the two essential sides of the argument. Heck, I couldn't even comprehend the fundamental argument *because no one is willing to state it!* We are so hands off.

The initial split that drove us insane - and resulted in humanity splintering into a million pieces - is the split between man and woman. It has led us down a long, weary road of finger-pointing nonsense. The misunderstanding is immense. The perceptions of the two genders must converge before we can fulfill our human destiny. There is only one sane way. The insane ways are all around you.

Our highly developed mind is well aware of the dilemma, even though we try to refute it.

It is the elephant in the room. It cannot hide in our subconscious and, yet, we cage it there. Our sentient awareness rebels against the hopelessness and helplessness to which we have surrendered. We are not just an animal. We are not 'just human'. We are sentient.

The issue impedes our fulfillment as a loving, honourable, dignified race of sentient beings guided by our self-respect and self-confidence which, believe it or not, we have the potential to fulfill. We have blocked ourselves from attaining the goal.

An unintentional deceit caused the disaster. It is an issue that the animal *has to* accept. Humans do not. We convinced ourselves we also had to accept the issue, long ago. Our sentient awareness has always known better. This has caused a disparity between our prehuman state and our heightened awareness.

Women view this aspect of life as inevitable and men, well, men, have been avoiding this aspect of life since the beginning many, many millennia ago.

Before you read the next paragraph, I ask you to ask yourself, "why did my brain just shut down?" Just in case it does.

How can a woman ever ask, "why can't you last as long as it takes for me to reach full-on orgasm? You know, that incredible feeling *you* get, when you eyes roll back in your head and, then, you immediately go to sleep?" Of course, I am painting the worst case scenario. The one in which the man is least evolved.

Men have been avoiding that question for three millennia.

There's a reason it's usually lights out. Not a good reason.

The woman's situation is difficult. How could a woman possibly know what goes on during coitus for a man? They can't. So, they shrug their shoulders and *try* to accept it. For ages, it just seemed inevitable. Men keep telling them they can do no better. Men are so wrong. In every way. It's easy - for a human. Sex has been cursed for the animal, not a human.

This is where that split personality came into play. Women accepted the situation as inevitable. Men were quite content to let it ride, even though it bent their humanity into a pretzel. It was too much for the undeveloped brain of our ancient ancestors. No one wanted to think about it or talk about it. That became a disastrous habit.

Our sentience has always known better. The lights should remain on. It should be the most wonderful celebration of sentient existence. Instead, we don't want to talk about it.

The man has been convinced all along, *because of historical inertia and the animal's instincts*, that he can do no better. He is so very wrong. Most importantly, it has bent the male gender's brain into extremely bizarre convolutions. They put on this act of masters of the universe while they haven't even learned to master their own bodies. Do you now see? It is nothing but compensation. Men know damn well they should be able to do better. Men have wanted to fulfill the woman's sexual experience, as designed, since the first day a sentient thought entered the male gender's brain. And they can.

It is also a causal relationship. More on that later. In short, it's due to an inferiority complex that has no reason to exist - any longer. It only existed because men always knew they should be doing better. They just couldn't figure out how. Then, they forced the issue into hiding before the intelligence could develop to overcome the failure of the animal.

Men never got over the initial assessment produced by the most ancient generation of humanity: there is nothing to be done.

You'd better believe that every man that has ever lived and attempted to love a woman has asked the question, "why in the world can I not last long enough to love a woman??!?!?!"

A man cannot love when he has not learned to love.

Men take, women give and it begins in bed.

Equality and equitable treatment of women will become natural when equal and equitable loving coitus is natural. Both genders suffer until it is so.

The current state has the tracks of the animal all over it.

The animal continues to cringe in a corner and tell us that there is nothing to be done about it.

To attain loving coitus, all we ever needed to do was utilize our clear-headed, sentiently conscious awareness. It was the clear head that was missing.

Our sentient intellect has to intervene. There is no clock on the act of coitus for a sentient being, other than exhaustion.

A man's full control of his own body during coitus takes a great deal of insight, *not* a great deal of effort. I've taken care of the necessary insights. I have no fear of persuading men to fulfill their unconquerable desire to be human enough to love a woman as designed, once they realize it is possible. Only the clutter of our past intervenes.

It will become easier, generation by generation, as the human instinct to love begins to take precedence.

The instincts of the animal currently rule both the mind and the muscles. That realization was far beyond the mental scope of our first sentient ancestors.

It does not require an insurmountable effort, though certainly a level of human determination and discipline. Any human male can handle the effort. It's like riding a bike. Making it an olympic event defeats the effort before it begins.

It is all about *not* using certain muscles (see Details).

There is no way the limited scope of a newly emerging sentient race could have coped with the question without a ready answer and, yet, the answer is not that simple.

So, the question was buried beneath the detritus of utter nonsense, frustration, anxiety, misery, and the ongoing destruction of our sentient state.

As our sentient awareness grew, the pile of nonsense grew apace to keep the question buried in the subconscious.

It's not terribly complicated to overcome the limitations to coitus brought about by the instincts of an animal. *But, it is nearly impossible to face the issue and seek resolution.* Coitus is too important to the ongoing survival of a race to be confronted as a failure without success at making it a loving event in sight.

We have been avoiding the issue for so long because we were so certain there was nothing to be done. That has distorted everything. No other resolution can compare to loving coitus.

A perfect example is the premature ejaculation studies. What is there summary judgement? If you last two or three minutes you're good. Do you see the defeatism? Do you see the acceptance of failure? Do you see the hidden lie? Do you see the animal peeping through? Do you see the excuses, the self-justification for failure? Do you see the inferiority complex and its compensation? Do you see the preposterous master of the universe? "That's the best that can be done. We wash our hands of it. Sorry about that, women, but it's just too much for us. You're left high and dry. We are masters of the universe but not our own bodies."

Do you see the root issue here? We are a sentient race. We cannot deny our sentient awareness. We *know* there is something missing. We can't deny it and we haven't been able to face it. We *know* we should do better. We know we *can* do better. Somewhere deep inside of every man, we *know* it is possible.

All we need do is think it through to realize that, of course, a sentient, *thinking* creature can do better.

Do you see how this has prevented us from developing our powers of the mind? We shut our minds down a long time ago in order to avoid this very issue. By doing so, we remain little more than a smart animal that is far too capable for its own good.

It's no more difficult to last as long as she desires than riding a bike or learning to talk. It's just that we have been so afraid to face the issue and try.

We have let nonsense clutter the scene. We cringe at the thought that we can never succeed, so the question remained buried. We feared that we were bound to the animal beyond any hope of improvement. We became hopeless and helpless.

It just takes a *lot* of insight, which I have provided (you are welcome), that our ancient ancestors were not equipped to ascertain. While the failure is unaddressable for an animal, it is addressable for a sentient, thinking, human being.

It is nice that some men have gone so far as to find other ways in which to provide pleasure for a woman. But, keep in mind that there are plenty of men left that think it's "icky". Very insightful, very human of some to assure the woman's pleasure, even though it took almost three for a few men to address their failure in this alternate way.

But, here's the kicker. I had a conversation with a guy that responded, "but I go down on her and she is totally satisfied!" I had to ask, "but are *you*?" No response. We know we can do better and it sticks in our throat.

The worst, of course, are those that have remained deluded into believing they are masters of the universe, even though they are not even masters of their own bodies and never, ever attempt to find an alternate way to achieve *mutual* sexual fulfillment.

It remains all about them. That is an unmitigated disaster.

I can envision a world in which every man finds some way to satisfy their partner and love flourishes to some extent. I am also certain, though, that some remnant of the animal would remain.

Even if every man alive could be convinced that some form of mutual pleasure is better than not, the lack of loving coitus would remain a problem. *We are sentient!* It is just ridiculous to believe we cannot perform loving coitus. It's not even a matter of whether a couple wants to perform loving coitus. It is that a sentient being should be able to perform loving coitus.

There may remain good reasons for a couple to use a substitute form of making love other than loving coitus but the certainty of failure of loving coitus is not one of them.

We *know* we should be able to experience loving coitus. It's like a hole in our brain that needs to be filled. If there is some rational reason for a substitute, then so be it. Buy, lying to ourselves is not one of those reasons.

Long ago, it became accepted that men were just going to continue to be lousy at coitus and humanity would remain an undisciplined monster. The two thoughts never converged.

Our humanity is cut down in its prime with every generation as it reaches puberty and finds something missing.

Only because we have never opened up about this issue! The animal's answer is to claim two minutes is success and move on. The sentient being will always ask why *unassisted* loving coitus is not working right, until it is.

Once that is answered, the human, sentient reaction will make loving into a work of art for both participants and we become a loving race of sentient beings.

Here's another sticking point. How do I convince you that we are meant for so much more. That it is the natural right of a sentient creature to retain its honour, integrity, and dignity instead of seeing it all go to pieces around puberty? How do I convince you that honour, integrity, and dignity are built in for a sentient creature, not developed through training? It is torn from our grasp, with each generation, by our inability to attain our fulfilled sentient, loving state.

A sentient creature evolves to seek truth. Our higher intelligence makes that possible. We try to correlate what we perceive with what we comprehend. We seek clarity.

When we not only don't achieve clarity but bury a question, we are not acting sentient. We are not acting honest.

In this one instance, long, long ago, we reverted to an animal. We left our potential for fulfillment lurking in our subconscious. Not only did we not resolve the issue, we wouldn't face it openly.

I hope I have finally succeeded. I hope I will get through to some. I know it is a challenge for all.

My two biggest concerns are 1) getting through to you without triggering one of the many alarms our conditioning has developed over the millennia in order to avoid raising the matter from our subconscious into our conscious awareness and 2) not going into a frenzy trying to convince you.

Men will not learn to love from the bottom of their hearts - like the best of women do - until they learn that they can easily love a woman physically in the most natural experience possible.

Fulfilling the experience that fulfills life in more ways than an animal can begin to imagine is what will make us human.

I have to stress this. It is not about a single man or group of men learning to love. That is not enough to transform the human *race*. It is not about each and ever man succeeding. It is about each and every man *knowing* he can succeed at loving coitus because he is a sentient, thinking, human being.

Humanity needs to know it can perform the most loving act of existence. It has to become part of the human consciousness. *Then*, we become human. It is not about men succeeding *by any means possible*, like taking a pill. An animal can take a pill.

How does a person love when they cannot express that love fully in a sentient manner? How does a sentient race survive without learning to love?

I've done everything I could to point out (see the chapter on Details) how, and the reasons why, it is possible for a man to last as long as necessary. That was my first imperative.

My only remaining question is what will it take for humanity to become convinced that any man can learn that he is master of his own body? I know my own success and detailed explanation, on its own, will not be enough.

I can only hope humanity can see what the ongoing failure and, more importantly, our unwillingness to clarify the situation openly, has done to our overall thought processes.

Make no mistake, the sexual studies have not verified anything. They started with the precept that there was nothing to be done.

All I can say is it worked for me and I am no one special in that department, believe me. I even had a few additional obstacles to overcome that few men would.

Yes, it will take a level of discipline, commitment, and effort, on the man's part, especially the first few that finally open their eyes and try, but it is the only way the male heterosexual human turns into a man rather than a rutting beast.

Discipline is crucial. Thinking is crucial. Both are sentient traits. It is what makes a human male a man (and I don't mean the toxic caricature of a man that is so often on display today).

Training Pavlov's Dog to act human is not good enough. The toxic caricature of the male gender is the reactive result to that effort. It is the difference between outside force an internal acceptance. It is the difference between acting out the part of a human and actually being human.

I am going to rely on the previous books to cover so much that I won't mention here, if you care to go further in your understanding. It is not really necessary. All that is necessary is to understand that humanity has to open its eyes, admit that coitus is not working as a human would desire, make the attempt, and, finally, become human.

For myself, getting past all of the delusions was much more difficult than learning the mechanics of loving. I hope I have made the former much easier to transcend and made it apparent that the latter is an easily acceptable effort. The younger the man is, the more easily he will adapt to loving coitus.

Details

Does it surprise you, men, that you can do so much better at coitus than your ancestors that have remained so tightly coupled to the animal's way of thinking through cajolery and self-enforced delusions?

Below, I make two attempts to make it clear how and why a man can learn to last as long as she desires. I am uncertain how to combine the two attempts. As I have said, it is so simple that words will not be needed in the near future. We only need to get over the hurdles of nonsense we have adopted for three millennia. One generation free of the nonsense and we will be on our way. It is as easy a riding a bike or learning to walk. It is only the mindset of an animal that impedes our progress. Do not underestimate the damaging effects of that mindset.

It may take everything a man has to get over the hurdle of lies. It will take very little for a young man to set aside the habits of the animal that have made every generation before him fail.

So, I will leave both sections without trying to combine them.

The Leap Never Taken

If any man has ever taken the time to think instead of scurrying into the darkest corner to hide from his shame, he would realize it is not *his* shame.

It might have been an animal's shame, but they are too witless to do anything about it, even if they are aware of the failure. Who knows? It might be that they rue the failure, as well.

For a human male, though, he has enough sense to think, if he is only willing. He is not witless. He is very, very aware of his failure and does everything he can to avoid thinking about it. *That* is a problem. He has been trained to do so.

He has been discombobulated by the inertia from the past. The hopelessness was passed on to him.

Everyone is convinced that the man is on some kind of a countdown clock when it comes to coitus. Sure, the clock starts ticking for an animal or a human male *that doesn't think things through* as soon as he penetrates.

Every man has the evidence right in front of him that the clock can go into suspended animation. Any man worth his salt has, errrr, taken care of things for himself, on occasion (rather than having it happen at an embarrassing, inopportune moment).

Did you ever notice how difficult it is to even get the clock started in such a case? There's a reason for that and it hints at why that clock should be completely under the man's control.

Of course, you will say, "but that's not the same!" *Exactly*.

There are actually a few differences between rehearsals and engaging with a woman.

One difference is that one cannot tickle themselves. That is, essentially, what does *not* happen during 'rehearsals'. That is part of what makes skin on skin such a glorious event, unmatched by anything else in life. The erogenous zones, not to mention every nerve anywhere it the body responds to skin on skin. Essentially, the coital act has elements similar to the two well-defined ticklish responses in other areas of the body. In this case, the muscles triggered are those in the crotch. That is critical.

There are also other differences, as well. They all add up to a man being able to make love the way he has always dreamed *if he takes the time and effort to think it through*.

Another difference is that, when engaging a woman, there is movement that is usually missing when one 'rehearses'. That movement, when studied, makes it clear what is happening, why the animal has *no* control *and* why every human can, if we just quit shutting the whole conversation down.

An animal operates by instincts. Let me interpret "instincts" for you. Instincts is performing an act without thinking. It is doing something the same way it has always been done *because you are not thinking it through*.

Sound familiar? It should. It is the overall way in which we have operated for millennia. Like a witless animal.

One mistake *the animal makes* should be glaringly obvious but, somehow, it seldom really hits home. There is a driving urge for a man to dive as deep as he can. It is often even encouraged by the woman. It is a really good feeling.

Unfortunately, it triggers the *approach of climax* for the man in short order. Save it for the grand finale. It will be the finale, whether it is grand or not.

If you remain an animal, it is called rutting. It is done without thinking. It is *done* way too early for a human.

The musculoskeletal structure is set up to begin the discharge process when you dive deep.

In essence, it is all about the glands in the crotch that retain the vast majority of the fluids that make up the discharge of semen. When those glands are squeezed, Bang! You're done.

Even without the instinct to deep dive, there is one more instinct that must be avoided. This one is a little more subtle.

The muscles in the crotch, surrounding the glands, when flexed and released, squeeze the glands. Those muscles do not need to flex and release. This will take a little more effort than "don't do that". You will actually have to think it through.

There are two ways this 'pumping action' can happen. Both are nothing more than the instincts of the animals that came before us that can be overcome easily - *if you can think like a human*. Animals perform those actions because they *can't* think. We perform them because we have not thought.

Men don't think it through because they never realized it was nothing more than instincts. No one told them any different. Well, I'm telling you, DON'T.

The two actions? First of all, the muscles in the crotch are flexed during the movements of coitus *without thinking*, thus squeezing the glands. The muscles in the crotch *are not necessary for movement*. They are only flexed during movement because we never think about it. Any bodily movement can easily be accomplished without flexing the muscles in the crotch.

With just a little forethought and practice, a man can avoid using the muscles in the crotch during coitus - until it is time. The muscles in the legs, back, torso, etc can provide all necessary movement *without* the use of the pelvic muscles.

It takes practice, of course, but the crotch muscles are independent of movement. You don't flex them because they are needed for movement. You flex them because of instincts. No one ever really thought about it because we were all acting like scared little children unwilling to look under the bed.

Secondly, the 'ticklish' (erogenous, if you prefer) response mentioned earlier. The muscles in the crotch get almost no exercise. While performing the particular movements of coitus, it is dangerously easy for those muscles to inadvertently and unnecessarily spasm in response to the mind-bending erotic 'ticklish sense', if you are not in control of your muscles. It is a challenge to avoid flexing those muscles due to this, but not really even difficult.

It is far from impossible. It's just something that no one has ever spent any time studying. So much for 'mystery'.

It takes a *little* forethought and a *little* regular exercise of those muscles in one's crotch to be able to prevent the unwilling muscle contractions.

That's it. The exercise makes the muscles more supple. The forethought and practice make them responsive to your commands (including unresponsiveness to the ticklish reaction, except as desired). That's all there is to controlling those muscles and, thus, controlling ejaculation. So much for mystery.

I came up with two terms: "don't twerk" (i.e. don't dive deep) until the lady sings (i.e. is ready for her own climax or climaxes) and "don't jerk" (i.e. don't flex those muscles in the crotch; the most challenging may be when changing directions of the stroke) to make the concepts easy to remember. I know, corny.

If you are not enraged by the fact that this has been there all along and, somehow, your ancestors never got a clue, don't feel alone. I was burned for a lifetime. I hope you catch on sooner. My fury, once I discovered the dodge game we have played, nearly consumed me.

As one learns what they are doing, unless the woman is doing her best to catch you off guard (which may become a great game to see who can outlast whom), it becomes easy to last as long as one desires. Can you imagine coitus as a loving, fun event?

There is, of course, a lot of fine print. It is no big deal. Only one more regarding early discharge. It's also the easiest to understand. If the glands are overfull, nothing it going to stop them from being squeezed and, thus, beginning discharge. No different than the bladder being in the same condition.

The other fine print is the woman's anatomy. If you want to be her lover, if you want to make love to her, if you want her to climax, you will also want to learn a little about her anatomy. I cover that, to a great extent, in some of the other books.

I will mention the most important, though. The nub of the clitoris, the most erotic response zone on a woman is located *outside* and just above of the vagina. It should be easy to stimulate as long as you know where it is. It is usually a half-inch or less from the opening. It is all about your positioning.

If you aren't paying attention, you may very well miss stimulating it at all. The rest of the massively erotic clitoris? Within *an inch or so, just inside* the opening.

Why, then, is the deep dive so enticing for both the man and the woman? Ummm, it is an incredible feeling? *As is mutual orgasm* (not necessarily simultaneous, though that might make a nice goal). Save it for the grand finale. It's the icing on the cake for the humans that finally can make love.

The other aspect that I will stress, I am certain will need no emphasis once we become human. A man is easily aroused. A woman, at least in our prehuman condition, not so much. Your efforts to arouse her need to be in everything you do. The way you touch her, the way you look at her. The way you communicate with her. In essence, the way you romance her.

I don't worry about this too much. It isn't that men can't conceive of what love means and how to achieve it, in all its glory. It is only unremitting failure to last long enough to count that has done men's attempts at romance to fade.

Romance is far more than the effort taken to get her in bed the first time. It is the effort that should last a lifetime amidst the incredible backdrop of love.

Oh, goodness! You will be able to spend a lifetime gazing into her eyes as she transcends this existence right along with you. I am so jealous! ... In a good way. ;~j

That was the latest attempt to explain. This is my old self raging, to some extent, at the stupourdity of the ages along with a bit more analytical approach as it leads into Details.

Leading into Details

All of the books that I have written over the last twelve years are about the fact that men never learned to transform the act that creates life into an act that also creates love. That has resulted in damage to the human race's development as a sentient race.

The male *gender, not a few individuals*, needs to learn that men can learn to love - easily. It needs to become firmly implanted into the brain of the human species. In other words, the human consciousness must become certain of the fact.

Have you had "that talk" with your father yet? How did it go? Did he fumble around and never say anything of import? Was he utterly relieved when you told him, it's okay, dad, I know all about it. Which you didn't.

Don't hold it against him. I'm not sure any man has really known how to love a woman physically before. They've usually known what the animal passed on to us. Rut. Stick it in and get it over with. Maybe think about baseball. Some may have actually stumbled onto a way to last long enough. That is not the same as the human potential to completely understand the situation and overcome the limitations of the animal with full awareness.

I am all about simplifying what I am trying to say. Even so, it is just such a complicated picture - in that we have been taught wrong about essentially everything for three thousand years - It has taken me writing eleven books to understand thoroughly and explain. I am on my twelfth and final book.

We have made a mess of our sentient aware existence.

The easiest part to understand is how to love a woman physically in the most elegant manner possible. The loving and human version of coitus. It is the implications, obfuscations, and refutations regarding this uniquely human, sentient experience that has made the rest so complicated.

The saying goes that men want sex and women want love. That portrays the dilemma poorly. Men *settle* for sex, in utter frustration, because they have not been able to fulfill the act of love the way they have always desperately desired to do and Nature always intended to make a unique sentient experience.

This is about how a man learns he can last long enough to make coitus a loving, human, sentient, fulfilling event. This is all about how a man learns that he is not held hostage by an animal's instincts, low grade thinking, and a dim-witted brutish approach to life. This is all about how a man learns that he is not just an animal.

A man does not differentiate himself from an animal until he realizes that he can love. That is unique to humans and loving coitus bridges the gap. He doesn't learn to love fully until he can express that love in its physical form in the way Nature provided. Anything less is a disappointment. It is the only purely human sexual act. Eye to eye, celebrating life and love.

Early male humans equated themselves with animals and conducted themselves as such. They took a craven approach to life that has remained, in great part, to this day.

Today's male humans remain mystified by their failure. They have accepted it as such because that is how it has always been. The leap to see beyond the paradigms that broke our humanity are formidable. The act itself is simple.

I've learned a lot since the initial insight of "Don't twerk or jerk until the lady sings" and made it all available in most of the books starting with *Millennium* (my favorite).

Details

Number one. A man is not on a countdown clock in any way when it comes to coitus. Only animals are. That mistaken belief has stopped the male gender in its tracks for so long. The belief is that, once you are aroused and penetrate, the ejaculation process is off and running. That is true for an animal. It is not true of a human.

The huge mistake compounded by that belief is that the best you can do is hold on for dear life as you helplessly watch the tidal wave of ejaculate makes its way downstream. Let me be crystal clear. Any way in which you attempt hold back the tide, once begun, is bad. It can cause damage.

So, no, you are not on a clock and it is not a good idea to try to hold back the process of ejaculation, once begun in earnest. If you catch it early enough, you can stop all activity long enough for things to settle down. Some refer to this as edging. It works. Keep it in your toolbox for making love, but don't expect to use it except as you are learning to master your body. Forget master of the universe. Master of your body is far more fulfilling.

What really works is to understand why the process of ejaculation gets started and what can be done about it so that you become a master of your own body. It's not magic. You are only held back by the witless instincts of an animal that have never been investigated fully in any way before.

There is only one thing that gets the ejaculation process started. Squeezing the sex glands in the bottom of your crotch, your pelvic region. *That* begins the process. Nothing else.

What happens is that the glands gets squeezed by two events, the muscles and/or the musculoskeletal structure in the pelvic region. The squeezing can be avoided. They are squeezed due to following the instincts of an animal without even realizing it.

There is one condition in which there is no stopping it. It will not be stopped if the glands are overfull. It is already being squeezed by being overfull. The solution is obvious.

Otherwise, two primary instincts cause the beginning of the end. One is simple to understand and control. That is the effect of the musculoskeletal structure of the pelvic region. The other is overcome by mastering the muscles in the pelvic region of your body. It's not difficult to do. It was just difficult to unravel.

There is a desire to immediately plunge as deeply into that heavenly place, as you can. Save it for the grand finale. Doing so forces the musculoskeletal structure around the pelvic region into a position to squeeze the glands. It best to remain as shallow as possible until you learn what you are doing.

All of the woman's erotic nerve endings are within two inches or less of the opening, anyways. The erogenous zone with the most erotic nerve endings is the clitoral nub which is located about half an inch *outside* of the vagina. If you do no stimulate this clitoris button, it is unlikely you will be stimulating the woman enough to achieve own orgasm. More details later.

The one that is more difficult to comprehend is how the muscles in your crotch operate. The more I study it, the more convinced I become that within two or three generations, without all of the impediments that are currently thrown into our faces, like the bad habits acquired, the missing knowledge, and the expectation of failure, combined with a growing confidence by the male gender, will make it as easy as learning to ride a bike. It is a different effort.

You have to teach yourself to master those muscles and <u>*not*</u> *use them.* It is not difficult. It is just that we never tried because we always veer completely away from any thoughts on the matter due to the paralyzing fear of admitting failure.

The muscles in your crotch, your pelvic muscles, will squeeze the sex glands if flexed. *They don't need to.* Those muscles only contract because we never thought about it. We react like an animal without thought. Animals contract those muscles because they have the wit of, well, an animal.

The pelvic muscles have nothing to do with movement and, yet, during the movement of coital engagement, they contract and relax because we just don't think about it. We've never trained the muscles.

It's easy to prove. Try moving any part of your body by using only your pelvic muscles. You can't do it. They are not attached in that way. They are not muscles for moving. They are attached in a way that controls the output of bodily fluids. In the case of ejaculate, flexing the pelvic muscles, during tumescence, will start the process of ejaculation by squeezing the sex glands.

During coitus, you have to learn to move your body *without* contracting the pelvic muscles. It's not really a big deal, once you become familiar with the idea. It's not like trying to master the heart muscles (which also can be done to some extent; i guess some may even be able to stop the heart completely. it's just that you never hear about it because they are dead).

The pelvic muscles are not needed at all during coitus. It is just a matter of learning to move the body without allowing those muscles to flex. It may be helpful to use them when the woman says it's time to end it, but I am not even certain that it will ever be necessary. A deep dive is the best, most satisfying, and certain trigger. It is a nearly unavoidable trigger, which is why it is so commonly used before it is necessary.

This is why I came up with the phrase early on, "don't twerk or jerk until the lady sings." It's trite but it gets many points across. It points out, for instance, a most critical necessary point of control for the pelvic muscles. When changing directions, especially on the backstroke when you are withdrawing, it is *very* easy to let those muscles contract until well-trained. There is a tendency to jerk.

There is a third effect that needs to be considered but it is part of mastering the muscles, and not nearly as difficult. That is the erotic sensation. This is how the head of the penis gets involved.

The erotic sensations that can blow your mind can also trigger a spasming contraction of those muscles.

In essence, it is no different than the tickling sensation in other parts of your body. You can master the spasming by exercising those muscles, making them more supple and responsive. Don't freak out. It should take more more than a couple of minutes a day to train them, maybe less for someone that matures into his sexuality already knowing what to do.

Those muscles, essentially, have never been consciously controlled or trained and made supple. In fact, you can control the muscles reaction to tickling in any part of the body, if necessary. (i had a cruel older sister. i know). You can control any tickling sensation. If anything, it makes the enhanced experience more mind-blowing.

Once you master those muscles, some intriguing possibilities begin to present themselves. As I mentioned, the erotic zones of the woman are all very close to the opening. The most important, the clitoral nub, is about a half-inch outside and above the vagina. This nub, or button, has far more erotic nerve endings than even the head of your penis.

Without stimulating this, it is unlikely you will bring the woman to the point of orgasm. One has to pay attention in order to stroke the nub because of its position. One has to position oneself in such a way to stroke outside and above the vagina with the shaft of the penis. Make sure you know if you are stimulating acceptably.

The rest of the clitoris erogenous zone, the clitoral wishbone, surrounds the vagina just inside the walls of the opening. This is the other most important erotic zone for the woman.

While it is not a challenge to stroke with the shaft, bringing the head of the penis into contact with the clitoral wishbone is another level of stimulation for the woman. Do not even attempt it until you have mastered the basics discussed above.

Bang! You are now human. You should be able to learn to last as long as *she* desires. You can finally feel successful at the most transcendent act of human life.

I wish I could be around for the next hundred years or so, as all of this flourishes. I just know there are mountains more learning that will occur once men's terrible inhibitions, frustrations, and emasculations are shredded as loving coitus truly and finally becomes celebrated as it always should have been and is transformed into a loving art form.

It is the most important art form of love that will replace the grubbing ways in which sex is treated today.

I've had many women mention how it is all about the missing affection in men that is the problem. That is what drives women crazy and away. What women have never realized is that missing affection stems from the same problem.

How can a man not become inhibited in his expression of affection and love as he fails at the most essential act of making love? How can he maintain an affectionate demeanor when failing to express it in the most meaningful way in bed?

The man may feel utterly disappointed in the situation, as well as himself, feeling like he has already betrayed the woman he desires to show his love. Many a man will close up, once his failure to express his love in the most meaningful physical manner begins to sink in. It sinks in so insidiously many never even become aware of it. It can become a haunting feel that won't go away but, also, won't surface.

Yes, some overcome the shock. Some find other ways. You cannot tell me they are not disappointed all the same.

Men take, women give and it all starts in bed. It doesn't need to remain that way.

I will say, once again, kudos to guys that find some other way to satisfy their partner, kudos to those that have taken a completely different route to find love. I'm sure your affection is far more than those that never learned to love in whatever way is possible and works best for the couple. But, still, until loving coitus is a reality that mankind accepts and proliferates, it is a humbled existence at which any primate could succeed. Only with loving coitus do we separate ourselves decisively from the animals.

I mention exercises. It is in some detail below. There are also plenty of Kegel exercises available on the web. Just keep in mind that there are two parts to the exercise. The second will not be mentioned in any reference to Kegel exercises. The first is to exercise those muscles to make them supple and responsive. The *second* is to *not* exercise those muscles while exercising the muscles that are *meant* for movement in your thighs, torso, etc. in order to become familiar with the separation of efforts. I like my exercises better because they only take a couple of minutes.

Regarding masturbation (I explain more below). Do not abuse your member. That is even worse than any bad habits you can pick up from masturbation. On bad habits, do not let the habit of thinking only about your own causing your own orgasm during masturbation prevent you from thinking about the woman's during the actual event of coitus.

Your main goal *has* to be the woman's orgasm during coitus. You orgasm is assured, hers is not. Habits are hard to break.

I have left as much of my original details below because I am concerned that this is a difficult enough subject as it is. Reiteration in different words may help. I have not edited much.

Original Details

Men have always accepted that starting the process of ejaculation was impossible to avoid. Because of this misconception, it became a matter of attempting to *stop the end result.* **Big mistake.** That is far too late. It became something similar to an olympic event in most men's minds. More strength is not the answer. More control is.

The big picture is that the sex glands in the crotch, when squeezed, begin ejaculation. Nothing else. That's it.

Two instincts trigger the sex glands by squeezing them. It has been 'a mystery' before now. So much for mystery.

Men learned only to hold on for dear life *after* the process of ejaculation has already begun. That assures the two or three minute limit that is de rigueur in sex studies. A study of the anatomy and the characteristics of the act of coitus is much more enlightening. There is no limit.

The unfortunate results of uncontrolled ejaculation ends the act of coitus before it can ever become a loving, thereby, human event that creates the loving environment that is necessary to fulfill our humanity. Uncontrolled ejaculation is a disaster. It is prehuman. It is not necessary and highly destructive to relationships and the human race.

By studying the anatomy in the context of erection, ejaculation and some of the oddities of results of masturbation, it becomes clear. Squeezing the sex glands in the pubic area (i.e. the crotch, the pelvic region) begins the process of ejaculate discharge.

There are two instinctual reactions that cause the witless squeezing of the sex glands in the crotch. They is nothing more than the instincts of the animals that came before us. That knowledge has been shunted aside due to the overwhelming feelings of shame that were first encountered by the first fully awakened sentient intellect more than three millennia ago. Those instincts, when the shame is shunted aside and the intellect finally assesses the real situation, are easy to overcome because we are human, thinking creatures.

One of those instincts is as simple to overcome as it is to understand. Men don't twerk until the lady sings. Thrusting the pubic bone (crotch) forward to the furthest extent squeezes the glands decisively (i.e. twerking). The animal's *instinct* is to immediately plunge as deeply as possible. It just feels good.

In the case of twerking (undisciplined full forward thrust), the musculoskeletal structure forces the pubic bone into a position that squeezes the sex glands. It will invariably cause the beginnings of orgasm, and ejaculation in the man's case.

The second instinct is more subtle. The pelvic muscles *are not required for movement*. They have everything to do with squeezing the sex glands and controlling other bodily output functions. The pelvic muscles do not *need* to flex, unless desired, during the movements of sexual activity. When flexed, they squeeze the sex glands.

The other muscles in the thighs, buttocks, back, and torso, etc are the only necessary muscles for movement. The crotch muscles only flex due to the witless instincts of the animal. They don't do anything regarding movement. They are not used for movement, they just witlessly follow along.

It is just a matter of realizing this and avoiding using the pelvic muscles for the movements involved in loving coitus. This is what I term 'jerking'. It just takes practice.

The two endpoints of the stroke are the most likely to cause those muscles to flex inadvertently, which is where the term jerking originated.

It's not so much leaving them lax as *not flexing them*. Flexing and relaxing those muscles acts like a pump on the glands. The 'tickling' effect on the head of the penis cause the same results through spasming. Mastery of these muscles is key.

The muscle response (jerking) or deep plunge (twerking) squeezes the glands containing the fluids that begins the cascade to orgasm. Save the deep plunge for the finale, when *she* is ready. It will *always* cause ejaculation and orgasm on call within a very short period of time. You can learn how long, also, with practice. It can all be controlled.

Holding on for dear life is *exactly* what a man does *not* want to do as it amounts to *flexing the pelvic muscles*!

One additional critical point. If the glands are <u>already overfull</u>, squeezing the glands is unavoidable. The solution is obvious.

Only about two inches is required to stroke the woman's every erotic nerve-ending inside and out, while allowing the head of the penis to remain fully inside the vagina. The shaft itself strokes the most sensitive arousal point (i.e. clitoral nub) that is just *outside* and *above* the opening (by ~ one-half inch or less). The other major erogenous zone for a woman is the clitoral wishbone, much less than two inches inside.

Stroking the clitoral wishbone, just inside the vaginal opening, with the flaring portion of the head will also help stimulate the woman. That may be best saved for after you have learned the basics. The woman's twerking should assist her orgasm in the same way as a man. The two should discuss what works best.

Think on this. Now, once you both begin to achieve orgasm, you can leave the lights on and look into each other's loving eyes as you each achieve the transcendent state of orgasm.

Just be careful and go very slow until you understand 1) how deep is safe (it should be far more than two inches as you progress in your learnings) and 2) how to avoid contracting (or, worse, spasming) the muscles in the crotch.

An additional technique, if necessary, is to stop all activity at the first sign that you are becoming overstimulated until the sense of overstimulation is gone. It should not be necessary with exercise and practice but may be useful while still learning.

It is a learning process. We are human. That is what we do. That is what we are *supposed* to do. In the case of coitus, we have avoided the learning process, thus remaining a dumbfounded animal.

These points are straightforward and will become as natural as the instincts and animal responses that they replace within a generation or two of the time that humanity begins to succeed at love in its most essential physical form. Little real learning should be necessary within a generation or two.   It will be absorbed from the confidence of one's elders (which is completely missing today) and, maybe, a few minor insights that will be commonly known, like, "don't twerk, don't jerk, and exercise.   Become familiar with the muscles in the crotch and *don't flex them*. Make them supple."

The exercises are just as crucial for loving coitus in youth as it is for later in life. There are other benefits as you age, like not wearing diapers. The immediate advantages, even in youth, include making it easier to master the muscles and any untoward spasming of the muscles. It will take some slight effort and discipline, as well as exercise (two minutes!), to avoid flexing and spasming. Avoiding the deep plunge is just a matter of paying attention.   Now, you will be able to open your eyes to the one you adore while actually loving her in the best way.

I spend around *two* minutes (only two!) exercising those muscles daily, and, also, practicing *not* flexing them by only exercising the muscles that *are* necessary for movement.

On your back with knees flexed, swing your knees towards each other and away. Flex the pelvic muscles as you swing the knees towards each other. Relax the muscles as you swing the knees apart.   Thirty times, approximately thirty seconds.   This will make the muscles supple and help you become familiar with muscles. Then, flex another thirty times while swinging the knees in and out. In this case, leave the crotch muscles relaxed while working only the leg, butt, and hip muscles to get the pelvic muscles familiar with avoiding flexing while the the muscles meant for movement are working.   This could also be practiced during walking, sitting, or any form of exercise, though I found it best to be able to concentrate. I've also experimented with variations a bit.   One that is intriguing is flexing the pelvic muscles on one count, then leaving them relaxed on the next.

Then, I hold them for a count of five, relax, another five count, relax. Six of these total.

I would also suggest alternating between this exercise and doing them with the legs stretched out fully. Just swinging your toes suffice, in this case.

Another good, errr, non-exercise is standing knee bends *without* flexing the pelvic muscles. What is termed 'sexercise' would be a perfect time to practice this. Tai chi or squats work just as well.

In essence, you are trying to do two things. Condition the pelvic muscles *and* become familiar with *not* using them when unnecessary and detrimental to the act of loving coitus.

I really doubt this will be the last written on exercises to make it easier to avoid unwanted orgasms. I have already rewritten this a dozen times as I learned more and more. I expect there is more yet that others will discover once we remove the blinders.

Another caution. Self-stimulation (or dress rehearsals, or masturbation, if you prefer) needs to be done carefully for the man. If you abuse your member, it will come back to haunt you. *Do not inadvertently do so!* It will make it almost impossible to avoid the beginnings of ejaculation. There is no reason to abuse your member, *if you realize what triggers an orgasm*.

It can be difficult to achieve orgasm when, errr, taking the matter in hand, *because* the normal motions of coitus are *not* the norm during self-stimulation. Also, the tickle response is absent.

A person cannot tickle themselves.

Also, the urge to rush through can become a habit that follows through when attempting to last as long as *she* desires. Do not allow that habit to develop. It is really hard to break. If one uses something other than one's hand, it may be possible to engage the tickle response to some extent and begin to overcome it.

Abuse, which can happen in attempts to cause the tickle response, or rush to completion, will make the spasm response *extremely* difficult to overcome. *Do not abuse your member*.

Humanity should learn to approach masturbation unabashedly. It is far better than letting the lack of release get under one's skin. I'm not expecting that to change in a hurry. Once we lose our sense of shame regarding sex, maybe we will have a chance.

Also, don't let your child (either sex, really) be mutilated by circumcision. In the U.S., it is considered a Christian tradition.

IT IS NOT A CHRISTIAN TRADITION!!!!   The health aspect is also a crock. It is sadistic. It leaves scars.

There is no rational reason for the mutilation of circumcision (either gender), though there are many irrational, insane reasons.

A circumcised person can still achieve controlled ejaculation but it may be more of a challenge (I was circumcised).

More importantly, the biggest thing for me is that I am certain it leaves a psychic shock when they slice it away, no matter the anesthetics or sharpness of the scalpel. There's just no need for it. It is sick and sadistic. It is an animal reveling in causing pain.

I would say that, no matter where you are in the world, it would be worth checking before you have a baby.   In many places (the U.S. south), they will slice without asking.

Just remember, you are human. Of course you can control the muscles and your own discharge. Keep in mind that overfull glands means they *will* be squeezed and it will be over in a hurry. How you handle that is up to you.

Do not become discouraged if it takes a little while to adjust and make things work. At this point, it is all new. The older you are, the more time should be expected in order to adjust as there are more bad habits necessary to overcome.

You can now proceed to engage in loving coitus, mutual orgasm, enthusiastically in a human manner while gazing into your lover's eyes with the lights on. Love can finally mature into its sentient form. We can become human. Rather than a porn-watching subhuman race.   I apologize for concentrating on the men's issues but men have the most to learn, by far.

There is another point that I have not highlighted before. The closest I came was mentioning that, after men gain their confidence, their self-respect, the rest will come easily.

While that is true, it is not enough, at this point. During the transition into that state, there are a few things that a man will need to consider. After we are human, it will be as obvious as the Earth beneath your feet.

Not only does a woman's orgasm take some time but, at least at this point, so does arousal for many women. I think it is very possible that this, also, will change, once women become convinced that they, also, can expect to achieve orgasm during coitus on a consistent basis. Their enthusiasm may often even match that of the man.

The point is that, if a man does not take his time achieving the woman's high arousal, before beginning coitus, she may never achieve orgasm. I would love to see a book by a woman on these matters. The orientation for a man needs to change radically. It is not all about him. It is all about loving and giving, not just pleasing oneself.

For women, just make sure you are doing the opposite of what I've recommended for men and you should orgasm easily. Flex and twerk like crazy or as much as he can bear, which should improve over time. Relish the erotic feelings that cause the spasms to engage. Again, I would dearly love to see a woman write a book on the woman's sexual situation and insights.

I am becoming more and more convinced that, as we open up and become more comfortable with the change and the insights, we will learn a lot more.

All of this will become natural once we remove the blinders. We will no longer be in hiding, and we can look for further ways in which to improve the loving. I don't mean just the physical aspects, either. This book will become unnecessary soon.

As an example of the other aspects to explore further, I'll mention romance and, of course, foreplay. Those are other natural aspects of being human that have been inhibited by men's inability to love physically, his shame.

Once our natural desire to love is established and reinforced by men gaining confidence that they can love, the rest of our loving nature will flourish. This goes well beyond the intimate relationship, as well. Humanity can become a balanced, emotionally stable, rational loving race of sentient beings without the over-heightened paranoia and despair.

A few further notes as I progress even further. First of all, after six books I am annoyed to find that the excellent term that I had created, indefinitely delayed ejaculation, 1) is not unique, and 2) has been already adopted to cover the case of the poor man that can't ever ejaculate or, goodness forbid (yeah, still despise using the term 'god' in any form), might last long enough to pleasure his woman with orgasm.

Secondly, there is a lot better term: controlled ejaculation.

I haven't even touched on any of the subjects besides men lasting long enough that are crucial to making love. The rest of it will come easily, once men are certain that they don't need to fail at the most essential task: lasting long enough. In the meantime, though, as we seek our way, it is at least worth mentioning a few key points.

The rest is easy, if you consider it at all, but still worth noting. The emotional loving, the affectionate responses and attitudes; the romance, the foreplay, the loving attitude, the gentle, equitable treatment of women, the rainbow loving of women that has been lacking, all falls right out of what I have been explaining. Men must just put their shame behind them.

Also, remember, it is the woman that gets pregnant, not you. So, if coitus is off the table, deal with it. If you care for her enough, you'll stick around. Find some other way in which to achieve mutual orgasm.

I have to highlight, though, that there are other ways to *assure* (a condom is not assurance; the woman being forced to futz with her hormones by taking a pill is not, either, besides, futzing with her physiology and mental state) impregnation never takes place while engaging in coitus.

Admissions and extensions

Everything above in this chapter has been proved to my own satisfaction. It was more difficult than most any man should encounter from this point forward. That is the point in explaining all of this. The effort is not difficult. Just overcoming the brainwashing and avoidance of the issue was difficult.

In a number of ways, it was more difficult for me. I had no template. I was encumbered by all of the lies, misdirections, and utter suppression of the subject that have burdened mankind for millennia. I was also circumcised. I also had damage to the head of my penis prepubescence and, worst of all, I had abused my member.

I have now provided a basic template to move forward and avoid all of the pitfalls that I encountered over a lifetime *before* I realized it was all a sham almost too late to prove the case to myself.

I realize this does not prove the case for all men. That will take some time and effort by others to show that it is not an isolated case and expand on the basic template that I have provided. The point of the previous two paragraphs is to emphasize that I am no one special when it comes to making loving coitus.

Everything I have to add, from this point forward, regarding improving men's performance to the point that they are in full control of the body when it comes to controlling, errr, coming, and mastering their bodies has no proof, other than I have spent the last dozen years pondering it all and linking many, many obscure dots.

These insights came far too late for me to prove them out with any level of certainty. I have no proof they help but they are rational considerations, in some cases, extrapolations from previous insights *that did work*. Some, points below, are just clarifications.

I am way to friggin' old now to be able to 'test them out' with any validity. But, they make sense.

I have to start by stressing that we are only just beginning, so there will be a lot more to learn as we progress and shed the blinders.

Humanity never stops improving on anything that it (finally) takes seriously. Loving coitus will become far more than the clinical analysis that I have had to provide. It will become art. It will expand the art of loving into something more human, once the unnecessary fear and shame are put away.

None of this will be necessary at all as men begin to gain confidence in their ability to love.

It's just that hangover of deluding ourselves for three millennia that continues to concern me. So, the more thorough the explanation and understanding, the easier it will be for all men to get over the hurdle of the debacle of our past that has prevented the human race from loving fully.

On the topic of exercise, I want to stress *not* to follow any rule book. You may start with my suggestions but find what works best for you. I would be shocked in the extreme if people don't find even better ways to strengthen and train those muscles.

I lost along the way through the many books one interesting technique that can be used while learning to master one's body. Moving the whole body, rather than flexing the hips in any way, or not moving any portion of the *man's* body are two ways to avoid squeezing those glands.   I'll leave it at that for your exploration.   Then, the one element of spasming in response to the erotic sensation can be concentrated on.

Sometimes I think of it like this door that men have always considered locked against them. Now, as we push gently against it, we find it is wide open. Quit letting the fears of your ancient ancestors prevent you from realizing you are a human. You can love a woman the way you have always desired.

One of the most crucial points that I cannot emphasize enough is that it is about a man changing his focus and, thereby, his behaviour from that of an animal to that of a human. That is the real point of all of this. Men's humanity has been hampered.

The laser focus for every man needs to become that it is about *sharing* the love in its physical form. All of the myriad forms of love can flourish from that point forward.

This is where the discussion becomes more speculative. As I mentioned with twerking, it is the whole musculoskeletal structure that kicks in to squeeze those glands in your crotch. I think there may be another way in which the musculoskeletal structure can be persuaded to avoid putting pressure on those glands.

Men often have a tendency to point their feet at an angle with the toes away from each other.   I think there is a distinct possibility that one's toes being closer together than one's heels might very well cause the musculoskeletal structure to become less prone to squeezing the sex glands. It seems like it makes more room for the glands.

More so, as I studied it further, it strengthens the muscles on the inside of the thigh if one walks with the toes pointed slightly inward.

I have another exercise that I do. It is bending at the hips with the legs and back straight. When doing the exercise with the toes closer together than the heels, I can feel those back, inner thigh muscles stretching. I am beginning to believe that these muscles also need to be strengthened in order to make it easier to avoid using the crotch muscles during coitus. Just a theory.

I would appreciate a word if things begin to start working better for you. As I have said, I am the only verified person to succeed at this, so far.

Onward and upward

Men need not be ruled by instincts. We have so discombobulated ourselves that we are completely blind to the facts of life as a sentient being should perceive them. Do you begin to see *all* of the implications of men ruled by instincts?

I had to fight tooth and nail to get through all of the delusions. That's my excuse for my past rants in the other books.

Once loving coitus gets a foothold for a generation, it will be as easy as attaining puberty, riding a bike, or learning to speak.

It is really difficult to peer through the fog of delusions we created long, long, ago in order to 'keep the peace'. "Keeping the peace" never really worked. Women's effort to give men time to figure it all out has been a double-edged sword.

It probably kept humanity from destroying itself, but it also allowed men to shrug the issue away - except from their own subconscious where it continues to drive them mad.

"Don't think about it, don't mention it" became our mantra and our bane. It has never kept the peace in any way, shape, or form and blunted our sentience. We remain an animal thrashing through life with this massive hangover from the animal lurking in our subconscious, and hating every minute of it.

Like Pavlov's Dog, we have been trained to never think about the fact that men are lousy at unassisted coitus. We have also trained our adult selves to *act* human. That is not the same as *being* human. We have never attained maturity, adulthood.

We don't want to talk or think about it. It always remains lurking, despairingly, in the subconscious of both men and women. Always keep in mind what this does to our overall thought processes. It bends them.

Maybe I should to embellish that thought. One of my insights, long ago, was that humanity can be treated as a single individual (yeah, with a lot of quirks) that has attempted to mature into its sentience. This same thought process can be applied to any culture or *the two genders*. They can be treated as a whole for some purposes. A really good purpose is to perceive the overall mental state of each.

The male *gender* is mad. It may not show up in every single individual or may show up as a well-polished *act*.

Like Pavlov's Dog, women have tried to train men to *act* human. It could never work. A slight aside here. While I just said that the previous books are not really necessary, I think they are fascinating as I get into all of this in much more detail. It was the only route I could take to understand and explain concisely the tremendous complexity of three millennia of delusions that just kept building and building. I skim over so much here, like the difference between *acting* human and *being* human, the whole concept of laws and peer pressure to treat with Pavlov's dog. The ongoing pressure cooker that always explodes.

The male *gender* remains an undisciplined, mad, rampant animal, never attaining its sentient state. All because he furtively accepts the previous state of the animal that amounts to the failure to love because his ancestors, long long ago could do no better. Can you see the inertia? The blinds?

Anyone that tries to broach the subject finds it nearly impossible to ruminate with a clear mind. Our minds have been fractured in such a way that the subject of men's performance at coitus is driven by instinctual reactions that go back at least three millennia and, maybe, a billion years. I mention a billion years because that is how long sex-driven procreation (coitus, if you will) has been around. There is no way to even guess, one way or the other, what animals think about it all. Altogether, I can't believe they are all that pleased. And it shows.

Keep firmly in mind that a pill that allows a man to stay erect does nothing to resurrect his sentience or his manhood. It just emphasizes the animal.

Everyone thinks men are such dicks because of testosterone and 'being male' (whatever that is supposed to mean). That is the hopelessness and helplessness in action. So is the toxic caricature that so many men don as their reaction. It is compensation for the inferiority complex that remains.

The studies of "premature ejaculation".   I put the term in quotes because it is *so* misleading. Anything other than a man's full control of his own body and, thereby, his ejaculation, is premature. It remains an animal's act.

Couch it in any terms you like, if a man cannot last as long as *she* pleases, it is premature. No one, *no one!* has realized or even attempted to suggest that all men can do better. We folded that hand long ago. *What if they can't??!?!?!?!* We couldn't even face the question, so we accepted the answer that an animal is limited to and have excused the failure for millennia, relegating our sentient state to the wind rather than leaving the question open for a new generation of more highly evolved human beings.

The biggest barrier of all is that no one seems to be ready to believe that any man can learn love in its most essential, initiating, physical form. Instead, at best, they play-act out the part of a human, sentient, loving creature.

The reality has to permeate humanity's consciousness. Men can learn to love.

The subconscious

Everyone's subconscious has always had to contend with the failure of men learning to love in a physical manner without everyone taking the thought out for inspection. That may have been true even before humanity. Has the male animal always been disturbed by its lack? Has that been a force always moving animals towards a better existence?

Since we developed into a sentient, articulate species that wants to understand *everything*, it has had ripple effects on the male gender.

The primary ripple is the utter and complete destruction of the man's self-respect.

What makes this so difficult to discern is that it can affect a man' bearing in so many ways. He can thrust the realization away and become a toxic caricature of a man in his attempts to compensate. Or, he can surrender to the failure and fold in upon himself. He can strive obsessively to succeed in some other area in the abortive attempt to prove his manhood. Well, I could go on. All in all, it shows up in myriad ways. That makes it difficult to pin down.

The most prominent and awful result of letting this lurk in the subconscious, of course, is misogyny.

I won't go into the effects of all of this on women. It should be a straightforward extrapolation for anyone.

The one (lacking) characteristic that portrays the debacle that humanity has endured is best at describing the issue. It goes to the *heart* of the problem. The loss of self-respect.

I've mentioned, often, in the other books, that it is self-respect that opens the door to our sentient state. It is self-respect that completes the image of a sentient race. Self-respect and self-confidence are necessary to unleash all of those other virtuous, *respectable* characteristics of a sentient race, like honour, integrity, compassion, dignity et al that will epitomize the human.

Let's see if I can explain it in a different way than the, literally, thousands of ways I have already tried. Our sentience makes us very inventive. If we can conceive of it, we build it. Our *sentient* (i.e. fulfilled) humanity will discern the difference between what can be built and what should be built.

The subconscious is an intriguing aspect of human existence. It is where all of the nightmares reside. It is where we place any question or issue that we are not willing to confront. Most of the uncomfortable thoughts have one origin.

It is fairly certain that I am not the only one that has discovered what it takes to prolong the effort indefinitely. Whether they know the intimate details of the mechanisms involved (thinking about baseball is not) is uncertain, though unlikely. It is also uncertain whether anyone has ever understood (or, admitted) the massive ramifications of the failure to do so *for the human race*. Another legacy of the animal is that no one seems to think in terms beyond their own selfish means.

It is not about your own personal peace. It is about the peace of humanity as a whole. If studying your navel helps us achieve that, here's to navels!

The worst aspect of our situation is that the failure to bring coitus to a loving state bends men's minds into a selfish point of view. Men take, women give and it all starts in bed. If he has been trained well enough by the only truly sentient creature in existence, woman, he may overcome his offensive predicament, to some extent, but he never ever becomes a fully functioning sentient creature.

The male most often does his best to drag any woman down right along with him.

Liberation

We always talk about freedom. What do you think we really desire to be liberated from? If you think long and hard enough, if you look deeply enough, you will realize we have an unremitting desire to be liberated from the animal.

While our roots go back to the animal, our awareness is no longer that of an animal. *We know better*. We have enough wit to realize something is missing - and we buried it.

We also know what it means to be human, sentient, with all of those noble qualities and yet, we never have achieved that potential.

The disparity between our animal behaviour and our humanity is enough to drive us crazy. It has. Just look around.

Until we learn that men can perform loving coitus, like something other than a brute animal, we will remain a brute animal.

All of the liberties we desire roll up into one: we desire to attain our humanity. We want the freedom to be human.

Reality

The biggest difference between an animal and a sentient being is perceptions of reality. Humanity's is far more sophisticated and encompassing.

For an animal, it has to accept what it is given. It cannot even think in terms of changing any significant element of its existence.   The same lack that this is all about may haunt animals, as well as humans.   It's difficult to determine.   But, there isn't a damn thing they can do about it.

For a sentient being, it is crucial that it understands that our reality differs extremely from that of an animal.   The saying, "perception is reality" is nonsense.   Reality stands on its own. Perceptions that disagree are only delusions.

There is no excuse for the male human to remain incompetent at loving. That is an animal's reality.

We have followed the ways of the animal for far too long in so many ways. Roll over, play dead, and accept the inevitable. Or, the silly religious proclamation, "Wait until you are dead. *Then*, it will all get better."

We accepted a reality that is not consistent with our sentience. We accepted the role of an animal and reinforce the animal with witless conjurings, misdirection, and outright fabrication.

As far as I can tell, all of it, every single bit of that acceptance, was due to the acceptance of coitus as an animal's failed expression of love.

It was all a matter of inertia. It was the way that the animal life form had done things for a billion years. You might as well also call this instincts. Instincts of which the initial sentient creature, long ago, could not even begin to conceive or cope.

In our infantile stage of development as a sentient race, we relied on our animal instincts to make sentient decisions. Our sentient awareness had already developed. Our knowledge and wit, not so much.

We were scared little animals in the grownup world of sentience in which reality can be either manipulated, misinformed, and corrupted or accepted and improved upon.

Guess which way we went?

Loner, by circumstance

I am a loner extraordinaire. I wasn't meant to be that way.

In fact, I'm pretty convinced that those barriers that keep us separated, feeling like we are isolated from each other have more to do with haunting truths that remain dormant in our subconsciousness than anything else.

In order to shed all of the lies and attempt to reveal the truth, I *had* to become a loner. Anything beyond, "Hi, how you?" "How much is that?" and "Nice weather" leads to the distortions that inertia has created over three millennia.

All of those distortions lead back to the fact that we lied to ourselves a long, long time ago. For millennia, we have been fooling ourselves.

Inner peace for all of humanity

Sorry, but I'm about up to here with inner peace. The only way I will find inner peace is when *we* find inner peace. Anything less is a sham.

I was just reading something by the Dalai Llama. Rather than use his exact words, I am going to interpret for you.

"While the world continues to blow up around you because of some goddamned idiots, find your inner peace.

"There is nothing you can do to influence the world in a way that will improve it, so contemplate your navel. Just keep watching as those idiots destroy everything. Buy into the whole brainwashing that prehumanity continues to propagate: it's hopeless. we are helpless in an insane world."

Oh yeah, and when I say, "those idiots", "them", I mean every single fucking one of you.

"Keep your own peace and to hell with everybody else." I have a slight problem with that.

For that reason, I've written nine books and am working on my tenth. You really are idiots but you don't need to remain that way.

It is very interesting. I mention that I, perforce, became a loner. What I just realized was that I was hanging on to one last thread. It has been cut and it resounds in me because I still love her for everything about her.

She rages at the monster. She fights it every which way but loose. Because of that, she is hanging on to the belief, with inflexibility, that it all of humanity must remain hell.

What makes it more crazy is that she hates herself whenever she finds some form of loving.

That thread had to be cut before I could write (somewhat) coherently about inner peace. Not find inner peace. That won't happen until I can convince humanity that is is so much more than it believes.

I am still convinced that she is one of the few that could get it. She is the only one I know that has no delusions or illusions about our current state. The delusion that she retains is not unusual and it has nothing to do with our current state. All of humanity is convinced that we can't become human in short order, that our nonsense will drag on forever.

It is just a matter of pinning down exactly what went wrong so long ago and doing something about it.

I can still hear those old religious tenets rattling around in my head. Original Sin and the idea that there is something fundamentally wrong with a sentient creature.

The only thing wrong with our sentient race is that our enhanced awareness made apparent a problem with which we were not yet equipped to cope. We are now.

While, to the outside world I seem like the ultimate man of peace. That is so wrong. It is my contained rage at the bumblings of humanity that has kept me going.

Mistakenly, I kept hoping for just a tiny bit of love to fill in the gaps. That was just wrong.

It's just not possible until humanity becomes human. Or, at least one other person, accepts the possibility.

There are so many platitudes that gripe me.

"Dictators and evil geniuses always fall." So does everybody else.

I did find one that rang true (even though I'm a guy).

"I am a woman trying to live in a world that is gradually losing its understanding of what it means to be human" Shikoha

I could have shortened it to "losing its mind".

And, as you know I would add, "there's only one way to change that."

Root cause

I am trying to not beat around the bush regarding the root cause of our insanity. Of course, that has never been the real problem.

The real problem is that there are just so many ways to describe it, so many vectors that apply, and the many, many triggers that tell us never ever to delve into the subject of sex and, especially, coitus. While we have overcome the hurdle somewhat regarding talking about sex over the last century, we hesitate like crazy to brazen the subject of coitus. The firm belief is that all it can do is make you crazy. The truth is that we remain crazy *because* we have not delved into it. We remain crazy *until* we delve into it.

For nine books, I have been dancing around all of the triggers of humanity's fears and quirks created due to the failure of coitus and the overwhelming desire to *never* think about coitus, much less talk about it and, yet, still attempt to break out of the trap. Saying that is bizarre is the understatement of our existence. I am dancing around no more.

This first explanation is, maybe, most controversial but, also, most important. We will not be human until anyone that desires to engage in coitus can expect to consistently provide loving coitus. The ramifications of that single sentence could fill a book.

Does that avoid all of your triggers? I doubt it. No one wants to believe we are not yet human. Do you really believe this is the best a sentient race can do? I feel sorry for you, if so. Our salvation is ourselves obtaining our unfailing sentient form.

It still makes me sad that no one else can see it. It still worries me whether I can convince a single other human of the magnificence that humanity can be if we just open our eyes.

The Flower Power generation was pivotal. They made it thoroughly apparent to all that coitus was a complete bust. The limited insight developed, in its aftermath, that any way in which two people can find to share mutual orgasm is better than not. That leads to the obvious conclusion that loving begins with a mutually satisfying physical relationship.

Evidence

I have wracked my brain to provide evidence that this is all true throughout the books. As I have moaned before, I wish it were as easy as a mathematical proof. There are many aspects that are not easily evident.

I have provided proof that any man can easily last as long as *she* desires. I've done what I could in that area (see Details). That is not yet understood, but certainly true. The final proof will require a great many men learning to love.

Do I need proof that humanity is demented? Isn't it all around you? How do I provide proof that men are the originator of the demented state of humanity? Again, I see the proof all around.

The real question is why don't you see them? Why don't you see the connection? Why does, for instance, misogyny exist? Give me one good reason other than what I propose.

I have also explained why it is so difficult to recover from the mess. The distractions, we have actively pursued, over the millennia, increasing in complexity, provide the proof.

Maybe the best proof is that we have avoided confronting the *truth* regarding coitus for millennia. That is not human. That is not sentient. Instead, we call the subject, "distasteful". That is the animal obscuring the way. That is not what we do in any other instance, we seek answer. We seek the truth.

It is ongoing animal's brutishness, witlessness, and frustration showing. Do you see how this is evidence in itself?

The only potential alternative is that we are no better than animals and will remain demented. I can't accept that. Can you?

I have tried to show that the ongoing existence of the rutting coitus of an animal, rather than loving coitus, as prehumanity's mainstay for sex and the only sexually-oriented form of *procreation* disrupts the human condition to such an extent that 'prehuman' is a better term to describe our current condition. It is not a human condition. It is prehuman.

I don't want to get into details but, from overpopulation to destruction of the climate to wars, murders, misogyny, wealth inequality, and just about any form of crime you care to mention, it all relates back to remaining an animal. I'm sure, once we become human, there will be plenty of books explaining all of this. I've already written nine.

I think I finally have a very good handle on the most obvious evidence. As usual, it was pointed out in the very first book, but I didn't really emphasize it as evidence. I should have.

Why is it that we (up until the last fifty years or so) never wanted to talk about sex? We could hardly think about it. Even now, over the last fifty years, with everyone jumping on the latest bandwagon to talk about some form of sex, we *still don't want to talk about coitus*! We'll now talk about sex til the stars expire but *we don't want to talk about coitus.*

To interpret the view of many for you, it goes something like this. "Coitus is a bust. I want sex that is fulfilling and am willing to fight to make it so." A corollary is "Men are assholes. I wouldn't want to do it with a man for love nor money." From a woman's point of view (or a man that admits his coitus performance is not enough), this makes sense. I have a lot sympathy for the woman that says such, since there is *nothing* she can do about the dismal coital event. It's not her problem.

One glaring problem with this view is we do not understand what is wrong with men. It is not humanity that is broken. It is men. They will remain broken until we all face the truth. Loving coitus virtually doesn't exist and men suffer from their own delusions regarding the situation.

It's nuts. What should be the most glorious potential event in a human's life, the transcendental feeling *one* gets from achieving orgasm while looking into the eyes of someone of the opposite gender during the most natural, potentially love-inducing event imaginable that, also, by the way, *creates humans!* should be shared. Do you even begin to see the problem? In a word, "*one*". I even bold-typed and italicized it for you, in case you missed it.

Only one of the pair consistently achieves that transcendental state while engaging in coitus (the mainstay of sex, for sure, even now, after we broke all the barriers in order to find some way to achieve mutual physical love in an endless variety alternative forms) ... and, *still*, no one wants to talk about it. Doesn't that seem strange?

Kudos to the man that finds a woman that can achieve orgasm in under a minute or two. Kudos, but not enough. That is a point solution, not a solution for the race of humanity.

Let's be blunt. We have been ashamed of the act of coitus ever since we became sentient enough to recognize the situation. It ain't love when only *one* achieves the transcendental state. It remains a selfish act, just like the animal performs it. It creates a selfish atmosphere and mindset. Men take, women give, and it all starts in bed.

So, let's be blunt about the actual situation. It's sucks. Not just for the woman but for the man, as well. *This is important.*

Every man desires to love a woman. Duh. At least, he *starts out* that way. His mind becomes more and more damaged as it begins to hit home that he cannot. He begins to believe he is no more than an animal. He becomes selfish. He creates excuses. The only reason it has not torn us apart already is due to the unimaginable grace of the female of the race. She has tolerated what she never should. Because, the best women, are sentient.

No matter how much we try to hide from the fact, we are not sentient yet. We can't hide from the fact that animal coitus does not suffice for a sentient race. Our sentient state will never allow us to accept the animal's perspective. All we have ever done was force the failure to remain rattling around in our subconscious with no outlet. It has festered for millennia.

The Great Facade

This is where this book is going to diverge radically from the previous nine books. This subchapter is about the hardest truths. No dancing around the uncomfortable misperceptions that everyone has adopted because of the distortion to our sentient existence. We have been too afraid to confront the truth. This is all about the bare truth. My dancing around the truth has ended.

LGBTQ and the rest of the alphabet would never have become a means of splitting humanity into more shards, as it has done over the last fifty years, if loving coitus had existed. There are a number of reasons why this is true.

First of all, if heterosexuals were having a great time with coitus, they wouldn't care in the least what anyone else was doing in order to find love and achieve mutual sexual gratification. It is especially disastrous due to those couples that cannot admit that a female sentient being has every right to the glorious pleasure of orgasm. They cannot face the fact that most people need not be martyrs (the woman) or animals (the man). They can't stand the idea that true loving can be achieved in one of many, many ways. It is only the disaster of failed loving coitus, otherwise known as rutting, that causes all the trouble.

As hard as that may be to accept, that's the *easy* truth. Here's the one that, for many, will not be so easy to accept.

If loving coitus had been the common practice of coitus for the last hundred years (e.g., the Flower Power movement hadn't really blown it by only achieving part of the objective), there would be a lot less LGBTQ's in the world. I would expect, for a lot of reasons, there would still be LGBTQ, but it would not be nearly as prolific as it is today. It is all about love and there is no reason to believe that the essence of love is not flexible enough to encompass any combination that produces love, when presented with an unusual situation.

The one that hits home for me is the man that *knows* how lousy his coital performance is and, thereby, becomes hesitant. That man has been tagged as gay for a very long time. That many accept the title is not a surprise.

I know you don't want to hear it but it is the bald truth. Many, many, many people that turn to alternative methods to achieve love, do so because they could not find it in a heterosexual engagement. Loving coitus was not an option for most. There is nothing better than that loving touch and fulfillment, in whatever form. Unless, like me, one realizes that the true answer is something is missing from our sentient existence. As far as I can tell, I am the only one to realize that, so far.

There are a million reasons why loving coitus is not right for a couple. None of them should be that it's not possible for a man.

Another bald truth is that many that turn to L or G is because they find the heterosexual male repugnant. What no one realizes, or at least is unwilling to admit, is that the worst traits of the male heterosexual are *because* men fail at loving coitus. There seems to be no connection made between the awful characteristics of many male heterosexuals and his dismal failures. Believe it. It is so obvious that is is difficult to see how we missed it for three millennia. Who can overcome the destruction of self, the ego, the self-respect, caused by failing at the most loving event of a human life and remain human? Especially in the case where no alternative is provided for the woman's fulfillment which still happens more often than anyone suspects.

Anyone that fails at loving coitus (which is the vast majority of humanity) *has* to ask themselves if there is something wrong with them (both genders, by the way). They are not wrong but they are not right. They are wrong in that it is *not just them!* The woman is wrong if she thinks for a second there is something wrong with her (which so many do). It is the *prehuman* condition for nearly everyone.

LGBTQ are more honest with themselves than most anyone else amidst the crushing desire to receive a loving touch as well as provide it.

Many of those that found some other way were willing to go through indignation, disorientation, and despair to find some way in which to feel good about themselves and love another person by providing for their partner sexually, not only themselves.

Boldly, they desired human touch *and* human love and were willing to go to extremes to provide it. They should be proud. They were willing to go to great lengths in order to attempt to love like a human.

From this point, it gets really complicated to explain. Some heterosexual couples find some other way to achieve mutual bliss. Some folks would rather turn to more extreme measures rather than remain conscious of their failure at coitus or consider themselves unfit for heterosexual engagement because of their failure.

This is another point of confusion. If we were to rely on only those men that can currently achieve loving coitus, humanity would be out of business, extinct, until we learn that any man can learn to make coitus loving. Those that have learned the physical mechanics of loving are that few.

The point is *all men* must become aware that they are human and that they can overcome the failure.

There is nothing worse than the barren life in which the absence of any form mutual sexual gratification is accepted.

Believe me. I know that better than anyone. I have never been able to avoid *all of* reality.

Here is the hardest truth of all. Nothing can compare to unassisted loving coitus. Men, that is human males, that use their brain, cast off the delusions of the forefathers, accept the insights of a full, modern human, sentient unswerving, undistorted view of sentient existence, and take the time and discipline necessary, can love a woman the way that Nature made for us.

I did not want to use the phrase 'Nature intended' (which really annoys me), because that *implies* everything else is off the table (all those ancient triggers being set off, once again). That is only the connotations of a mindless beast that has been programmed for, at least three millennia and maybe as long as a billion years, to believe that coitus is only about making babies and babies are the only reason for sex, which is just stupid. That is only true for an animal (and not even them). We are human.

For a primitive animal, Nature requires babies and no confusion. The man had to achieve orgasm first to assure a proliferation of babies. For a sentient race, Nature expanded its repertoire. It added the amazing concept of love. That is initiated, in full measure, by mutual sexual gratification.

Coitus is not just about making babies for a sentient being. It is about making love, which is far more important for a sentient being in order to retain its sanity and not run amok.

It opens up the skies for a sentient race. That is why so many have fought so hard to achieve any form of making love.

One last clarification. It is not that every single human being has to achieve mutual sexual gratification. It is just that anyone pursuing sex, in order to be classified as human rather than prehuman, must achieve mutual sexual gratification. Otherwise, you are no more than an animal and a deranged and degenerate one at that. Too much brains and not enough heart, not enough love. No balance. The human race's consciousness must come to accept that loving coitus is the natural result of our sentient state. It has to pervade the human race.

Cascades

This was my last excavation.

I cannot begin to tell you the effort it has taken to see through all of the obstruction; perceive the many, varied perspectives that have little to do with reality. There is a reality and we have been avoiding sentient reality for as long as we have been sentient.

This is why.

Men confounded themselves when they convinced everyone, including themselves, that they cannot do any better than an animal at coitus.

The whole game of sentience went into a spin. That spin cascaded through our state of mind.

If you are still having trouble with these concepts, imagine a state in which all is right. A state in which a being exists amidst an awareness that it all makes sense, though it certainly had nothing to do with frolicking amidst lions, tigers, and bears.

Then, throw a joker in the game. Make him sentient. An inconsistency is revealed. Something no one wants to talk about.

Our presentient state currently lies in the tumbled confusion of that pile.

We could not answer the puzzle of loving coitus in a viable way. So, we *created* an atmosphere in which it didn't matter.

But, it did.

We are constantly aware of the reality. We can't avoid it and we can't accept it.

Wake up. It's foolishness to believe men cannot do better. We have been cowed into believing it for millennia. We manipulated reality by saying it didn't matter. What you see about you is the remains of the manipulated reality.

It is incredible that *for three millennia* the thinking human could not realize that it is just a matter of instincts that need be overcome. It shows clearly that here was a scam afoot. We surrendered. If that sentence doesn't disgust you, it should.

Nothing else was so important to our mental awareness, emotional stability, and sanity as loving coitus. And, *knowing* it should/could exist.

We could not accept the consequences of that thought. No wonder ancient man went crazy and dragged the female gender down with him. It is clear that someone early on understood the issue that had entered their minds. Pandora's Box tells the story well. Men couldn't do a thing about it *at the time*. ___But___, hope was left in the box.

They may have given that hope fifty to one hundred years before they became desperate. They couldn't sustain the state of contention very long. The Garden Of Eden was written shortly after Pandora's Paradox. They still knew nothing but needed a better answer *for the short term*.

The unexpected consequence was that is ruled far longer than expected because the answer given was: *don't think about it!* We are cursed for all time. Forget about it. Which we did.

The problem went even deeper than that, of course. Or, you wouldn't have every sexual institute bleating that there's nothing to be done.

Of course, everyone thought about it but the thinking was already influenced by, at least, three false vectors: 1) Men can't improve; 2) The best you can do is *try harder,* and 3) make it an olympic event. All of those made it virtually impossible to find the real answer. We looked at the whole thing just the way an animal would.   Oh, yeah, and, 4) don't ever *really* think about it.

Can you see how that would influence, over three millennia, *every major thread of thought that pervades the human race?*

The man accepts his failure in some way. If it is only in his subconscious, he doesn't even have to put words to it.   If it remains only in the subconscious (which, more than any other thought, it does; women too, I would guess - especially in those that are religiously programmed), it becomes part of a morass of questionable thinking that never sees the light of day.   That thunderous thought is at the center of all of the blurred perceptions of reality. We lied to ourselves once and continued to do so.

It creeps into the consciousness that something's not right. We'll do about anything to avoid the realization lurking there in the subconsciousness. And, yet, we face that issue and our lover, every day (or few days) during our active sexual span of life. It influences all of our thought processes. It is also a distraction to all of the other thought processes. We learned to cringe. We learned not to think.

Once we become certain of ourselves, it all goes away.

There has been a mountain of misdirection that has filtered through our consciousness since the beginning. All because, so long ago, we let one important, mind-dominating, thought become scuttled.

We learned to scuttle uncomfortable subjects anytime we could justify it. Just like justifying that coitus can't ever be naturally (unassisted) fulfilling. The truth of the matter is discussed in Details. Of course, men can learn to love. They're human, not just an animal run by its instincts. The justifications have gotten close to the point that no justification is required as we become more resigned to remaining an animal. Surrender.

It is a point of contention that made a wedge of nonsense grow into our distorted reality.

Our last three millennia have been nothing more than a scam men have pulled. They made the grave mistake of believing that lying about the situation would rescue their self-respect. They were so wrong. All it did was bury our sentience and their self-respect in obscurity.

Pandora's Paradox

I really wanted to put this earlier in the book. The problem is that, at first blush, to someone that is unfamiliar with my radical notions, it could easily get written off as preposterous. If you've gotten this far, you should see the links to the overall picture.

Pandora's Box has fascinated me for quite awhile. I've mentioned it in many of the books.

I prefer the term Pandora's Paradox. You remember the story, right? It's about hope and all the monstrosities that were unleashed with our sentient state. Pandora's Paradox states that earliest humanity was at a loss regarding some aspect(s) of our sentient state. The author was calling on future humanity to stay vigilant and pay attention. Hope remained. We did not.

The author of Pandora's Paradox was extremely insightful. The author could see that a coverup, a scam, was already beginning. We were going to try to hide what seemed shameful. Essentially, it was the most meaningful statement made in three millennia. "Beware! Be on your toes. A scam is about to be pulled over humanity's eyes. There is nothing to be done at this point in time, but there is hope left for future generations, if we

can avoid the blinders that will developed to hide from the truth."
We did not avoid the blinders.

It makes sense, really. Some could see the trouble developing alongside our sentience. Something was not right. That hasn't changed for three millennia.

At the time, we had not yet hidden the issue away so completely that no one could broach the subject. I'm pretty certain the author knew exactly what the problem was. Even then, nobody wanted to talk about it. It confounded our sentient state, and still does. So, she used a myth, a vague description of what was going on, since the blatant truth would not be tolerated.

Even then, the tidal wave of obfuscation was beginning to wash away nearly all of the evidence of the issue, as well as our sentience.

A discerning person, like the author of Pandora's Box, with a very sharp brain, could see that a certain predicament was too much for early humans to confront in her time. It was considered insurmountable to the great distress of half of the population. Sadly, it still is. Initially, it was just a bewildering phenomenon. By three millennia ago, it had already become obscured by active obfuscation. Its destructive force was clearly apparent.

Intuition took hold. She made the leap to realize it should not remain insurmountable. If humanity could keep an open mind long enough, it should be able to handle the issue, once it had matured to some extent. We did not.

Sadly, humanity could not keep an open mind. More and more, it crept into our thought processes and slowly distorted the male behaviour beyond recognition as a sentient human being.

It can be taken for granted that the author was pretty smart. Writing was nearly unheard of three millennia ago. I wish I could discern more. Was it a woman? Was it bigger than that? Was it a group of women? Was it a bold man looking around him at the increasingly horrible antics of his gender?

Humanity proceeded to obscure things further in short order. As one example, from the same roots of history and same general geographical region as Pandora's Paradox, is The Garden Of Eden. There is little doubt it was created as a contradiction to the bold truth of Pandora's Box. The Garden Of Eden is nothing more than a blatant lie, invoking a god to put it over.

The Garden Of Eden was a refutation of our humanity. The animal ruled and it was all women's fault.

How topsy-turvy is that? Men are the problem. They could not handle the truth, so they put the blame on women for realizing that men had a problem that they could not face.

Disgustingly, The Garden Of Eden proclaimed that it must be true because god said so???!?!?! (even though a man wrote the gross misrepresentation of our state) To paraphrase, "Everything was fine until we became something more than an animal. So, of course, the only solution is to revert to an animal."   I still remember seeing a painting of humans frolicking among lions, tigers, and other predators. Yeah, right.

Sentience is not the problem. Lack of knowledge to fill in the blanks of our sentient state has always been the problem. Since we scuttled the issue, the knowledge has never developed. Instead, we ran and hid like scared little children.

The intention of The Garden Of Eden was to refute what Pandora's Paradox suggested: there was hope that, at some future date, as our knowledge increased, we could overcome the foul stench of our animal antics when it came to sex.   Instead, it proclaimed we are cursed before we are born. Original Sin and all that. We surrendered without a fight.

The Garden Of Eden was a nail in the coffin of our humanity. Its intent was to lock the mind up and obscured the facts.   It worked.   The West has followed that nonsense for more than three millennia.   I am not certain what nonsense was used to cloud the issue in other cultures. Maybe nothing was required because there was no story of Pandora's Box to disturb the rule of the insane.

In explicit terms, Pandora's Paradox suggested that even though men are lousy at coitus, sooner or later, they could learn damn well how not to be.   "Some day" would not work for most men, so they burned it and razed its ashes.   They would be humbled by their failure, so they invented a world that does not exist. A world in which the male toxic caricature continues to grow. It won't go away until we accept the truth.

The intent of The Garden Of Eden was to confuse and obfuscate what Pandora's Paradox revealed. The Garden Of Eden is a directly distorted extrapolation of Pandora's Paradox for that very purpose. It's only intent was to obscure. How could men rule while having such a glaring *sentient* problem? More importantly, they wouldn't have the mad desire to rule and control everything around them if they could only control their own body and/or accept the bold truth.

Woman got blamed. The rest is history.

In some ways, Pandora's Box was a description of what happened during the blossoming of our sentience. The Box that Pandora was given contained our sentience which was released on the world, but there was a single drawback with which we were not prepared to contend. So, the issue was scuttled along with our sentience.

I am all about the hope.

No Masks

There is an existence for humanity in which there are no masks. It is right around the corner. It is filled with sentient beauty and love.

That doesn't mean you won't have bumps and bruises in life. It just means they won't break you.

I swear, I've gone over it a million times. We will stay just the same damaged species as we have been if we don't accept the truth. Nothing will change, just as it has never changed significantly for the last three thousand years. We will be having the same complaints three thousand years from now if men don't learn how to love.

Thank you for reading this book

whickwithy@gmail.com

I just thought it would be nice to reiterate the reason I use this photo. Considering I have spent the last twelve years attempting to form my knowledge and awareness into something that can convey all of the nonsense that we endure and how we finally become human, there has been a whole lot of snarling. The forty years before that, while I was just wondering what is wrong with the human race, it wasn't so bad.

Men need to join the human race.